ROSA MUNDI
AND OTHER LOVE SONGS

1905

By

ALEISTER CROWLEY

A Yesterday's World Publishing

Published by A Yesterday's World Publishing
Copyright © 2019 A Yesterday's World Publishing
First Edition 2019
ISBN - 978-1-912925-69-8

1. ROSE of the World!
Red glory of the secret heart of Love!
Red flame, rose-red, most subtly curled
Into its own infinite flower, all flowers above!
Its flower in its own perfumed passion,
Its faint sweet passion, folded and furled
In flower fashion;
And my deep spirit taking its pure part
Of that voluptuous heart
Of hidden happiness!

2. Arise, strong bow of the young child Eros!
(While the maddening moonlight, the memoried caress
Stolen of the scented rose
Stirs me and bids each racing pulse ache, ache!)
Bend into an agony of art
Whose cry is ever rapture, and whose tears
For their own purity's undivided sake
Are molten dew, as, on the lotus leaves
Sliver-coiled in the Sun
Into green girdled spheres
Purer than all a maiden's dream enweaves,
Lies the unutterable beauty of
The Waters.   Yea, arise, divinest dove
Of the Idalian, on your crimson wings
And soft grey plumes, bear me to yon cool shrine
Of that most softly-spoken one,
Mine Aphrodite!   Touch the imperfect strings,
Oh thou, immortal, throned above the moon!
Inspire a holy tune
Lighter and lovelier than flowers and wine
Offered in gracious gardens unto Pan
By any soul of man!

3. In vain the solemn stars pour their pale dews
Upon my trembling spirit; their caress
Leaves me moon-rapt in waves of loveliness
All thine, O rose, O wrought of many a muse
In Music, O thou strength of ecstasy
Incarnate in a woman-form, create
Of her own rapture, infinite, ultimate,
Not to be seen, not grasped, not even imaginable,
But known of one, by virtue of that spell
Of thy sweet will toward him: thou, unknown,
Untouched, grave mistress of the sunlight throne
Of thine own nature; known not even of me,

But of some spark of woven eternity
Immortal in this bosom.   Phosphor paled
And in the grey upstarted the dread veiled
Rose light of dawn.   Sun-shapen shone thy spears
Of love forth darting into myriad spheres,
Which I the poet called this light, that flower,
This knowledge, that illumination, power
This and love that, in vain, in vain, until
Thy beauty dawned, all beauty to distil
Into one drop of utmost dew, one name
Choral as floral, one thin, subtle flame
Fitted to a shaft of love, to pierce, to endue
My trance-rapt spirit with the avenue
Of perfect pleasures, radiating far
Up and up yet to where thy sacred star
Burned in its brilliance: thence the storm was shed
A passion of great calm about this head,
This head no more a poet's; since the dream
Of beauty gathered close into a stream
Of tingling light, and, gathering ever force
From thine own love, its unextended source,
Became the magic utterance that makes Me,
Dissolving self into the starless sea
That makes one lake of molten joy, one pond
Steady as light and hard as diamond;
One drop, one atom of constraint intense,
Of elemental passion scorning sense,
All the concentred music that is I.
O! hear me not!   I die;
I am borne away in misery of dumb life
That would in words flash forth the holiest heaven
That to the immortal God of Gods is given,
And, tongue-tied, stammers forth—my wife!

4. I am dumb with rapture of thy loveliness.
All metres match and mingle; all words tire;
All lights, all sounds, all perfumes, all gold stress
Of the honey-palate, all soft strokes expire
In abject agony of broken sense
To hymn the emotion tense
Of somewhat higher—O! how highest!—than all
Their mystery: fall, O fall,
Ye unavailing eagle-flights of song!
O wife! these do thee wrong.

5. Thou knowest how I was blind;

How for mere minutes thy pure presence
Was nought; was ill-defined;
A smudge across the mind,
Drivelling in its brutal essence,
Hog-wallowing in poetry,
Incapable of thee.

6. Ah! when the minutes grew to hours,
And yet the beast, the fool, saw flowers
And loved them, watched the moon rise, took delight
In perfumes of the summer night,
Caught in the glamour of the sun,
Thought all the woe well won.
How hours were days, and all the misery
Abode, all mine: O thou! didst thou regret?
Wast thou asleep as I?
Didst thou not love me yet?
For, know! the moon is not the moon until
She hath the knowledge to fulfil
Her music, till she know herself the moon.
So thou, so I!   The stone unhewn,
Foursquare, the sphere, of human hands immune,
Was not yet chosen for the corner-piece
And key-stone of the Royal Arch of Sex;
Unsolved the ultimate x;
The virginal breeding breeze
Was yet of either unstirred;
Unspoken the Great Word.

7. Then on a sudden, we knew.   From deep to deep
Reverberating, lightning unto lightning
Across the sundering brightening
Abyss of sorrow's sleep,
There shone the sword of love, and stuck, and clove
The intolerable veil,
The woven chain of mail
Prudence self-called, and folly known to who
May know.   Then, O sweet drop of dew,
Thy limpid light rolled over and was lost
In mine, and mine in thine,
Peace, ye who praise! ye but disturb the shrine!
This voice is evil over against the peace
Here in the West, the holiest. Shaken and crossed
The threads Lachesis wove fell from her hands.
The pale divided strands
Where taken by thy master-hand, Eros!

Her evil thinkings cease,
Thy miracles begin.
Eros!   Eros!—Be silent!   It is sin
Thus to invoke the oracles of orde.
Their iron gates to unclose.
The gross, inhospitable warder
Of Love's green garden of spice is well awake.
Hell hath enough of Her three-headed hound;
But Love's severer bound
Knows for His watcher a more fearful shape,
A formidable ape
Skilled by black art to mock the Gods profound
In their abyss of under ground.
Beware! Who hath entered hath no boast to make,
And conscious Eden surelier breeds the snake.
Be silent!   O! for silence' sake!

8. That asks the impossible.   Smite! Smite!
Profaned adytum of pure light.
Smite! but I must sing on.
Nay! can the orison
Of myriad fools provoke the Crowned-with-Night
Hidden beyond sound and sight
In the mystery of His own high essence?
Lo, Rose of all the gardens of the world,
Did thy most sacred presence
Not fill the Real, then this voice were whirled
Away in the wind of its own folly, thrown
Into forgotten places and unknown.
So I sing on!
              Sister and wife, dear wife,
Light of my love and lady of my life,
Answer if thou canst from the unsullied place,
Unveiling for one star-wink thy bright face!
Did we leave then, once cognisant,
Time for some Fear to implant
His poison?   Did we hesitate?
Leave but one little chance to Fate?
For one swift second did we wait?
There is no need to answer: God is God,
A jealous God and evil; with His rod
He smiteth fair and foul, and with His sword
Divideth tiniest atoms of intangible time,
That men may know he is the Lord.
Then, with that sharp division,
Did He divide our wit sublime?

Our knowledge bring to nought?
We had no need of thought.
We brought His malice in derision.
So thine eternal petals shall enclose
Me, O most wonderful lady of delight,
Immaculate, indivisible circle of night,
Inviolate, invulnerable Rose!

9. The sound of my own voice carries me on.
I am as a ship whose anchors are all gone.
Whose rudder is held by Love the indomitable -
Purposeful helmsman!   Were his port high Hell,
Who should be fool enough to care? Suppose
Hell's waters wash the memory of this rose
Out of my mind, what misery matters then?
Or, if they leave it, all the woes of men
Are as pale shadows in the glory of
That passionate splendour of Love.

10. Ay! my own voice, my own thoughts. These, then, must be
The mutiny of some worm's misery,
Some chained despair knotted into my flesh,
Some chance companion, some soul damned afresh
Since my redemption, that is vocal at all,
For I am wrapt away from light and call
In the sweet heart of the red rose.
My spirit only knows
This woman and no more; who would know more?
I, I am concentrate
In the unshakable state
Of constant rapture.   Who should pour
His ravings in the air for winds to whirl,
Far from the central pearl
Of all the diadem of the universe?
Let God take pen, rehearse
Dull nursery tales; then, not before, O rose,
Red rose! shall the beloved of thee,
Infinite rose! pen puerile poetry
That turns in writing to vile prose.

11. Were this the quintessential plume of Keats
And Shelley and Swinburne and Verlaine,
Could I outsoar them, all their lyric feats,
Excel their utterance vain
With one convincing rapture, beat them hollow
As an ass's skin; wert thou, Apollo,

Mere slave to me, not Lord—thy fieriest flight
And stateliest shaft of light
Thyself thyself surpassing: all were dull,
And thou, O rose, sole, sacred, wonderful,
Single in love and aim,
Double in form and name,
Triple in energy of radiant flame,
Informing all, in all most beautiful,
Circle and sphere, perfect in every part,
High above hope of Art:
Though, be it said! thou art nowhere now,
Save in the secret chamber of my heart,
Behind the brass of my anonymous brow.[1]

12. Ay! let the coward and slave who writes write on!
He is no more harm to Love than the grey snake
Who lurks in the dusk brake
For the bare-legged village-boy, is to the Sun,
The Sire of Life.
The Lover and the Wife,
Immune, intact, ignore.   The people hear;
Then, be the people smitten of grey Fear,
It is no odds!

13. I have seen the eternal Gods
Sit, star-wed, in old Egypt by the Nile;
The same calm pose, the inscrutable, wan smile,
On every lip alike.
Time hath not had his will to strike
At them; they abide, they pass through all.
Though their most ancient names may fall,
They stir not nor are weary of
Life, for with them, even as with us, Life is but Love.
They know, we know; let, then, the writing go!
That, in the very deed, we do not know.

14. It may be in the centuries of our life
Since we were man and wife
There stirs some incarnation of that love.
Some rosebud in the garden of spices blows,
Some offshoot from the Rose
Of the World, the Rose of all Delight,
The Rose of Dew, the Rose of Love and Night,
The Rose of Silence, covering as with a vesture

---

[1] This poem was issued under the pseudonym of H. D. Carr.

The solemn unity of things
Beheld in the mirror of truth,
The Rose indifferent to God's gesture,
The Rose on moonlight wings
That flies to the House of Fire,
The Rose of Honey-in-Youth!
Ah! No dim mystery of desire
Fathoms this gulf! No light invades
The mystical musical shades
Of a faith in the future, a dream of the day
When athwart the dim glades
Of the forest a ray
Of sunlight shall flash and the dew die away!

15. Let there then be obscurity in this!
There is an after rapture in the kiss.
The fire, flesh, perfume, music, that outpaced
All time, fly off; they are subtle: there abides
A secret and most maiden taste;
Salt, as of the invisible tides
Of the molten sea of gold
Men may at times behold
In the rayless scarab of the sinking sun;
And out of that is won
Hardly, with labour and pain that are as pleasure,
The first flower of the garden the stored treasure
That lies at the heart's heart of eternity.
This treasure is for thee.

16. O! but shall hope arise in happiness?
That may not be.
My love is like a golden grape, the veins
Peep through the ecstasy
Of the essence of ivory and silk,
Pearl, moonlight, mother-milk
That is her skin;
Its swift caress
Flits like an angel's kiss in a dream; remains
The healing virtue; from all sin,
All ill, one touch sets free.
My love is like a star—oh fool! oh fool!
Is not thy back yet tender from the rod?
Is there no learning in the poet's school?
Wilt thou achieve what were too hard for God?
I call Him to the battle; ask of me
When the hinds calve?   What of eternity

When he built chaos?   Shall Leviathan
Be drawn out with a hook?   Enough; I see
This I can answer—or Ernst Haeckel can!
Now, God Almighty, rede this mystery!
What of the love that is the heart of man?
Take stars and airs, and write it down!
Fill all the interstices of space
With myriad verse——own Thy disgrace!
Diminish Thy renown!
Approve my riddle! This Thou canst not do.

17. O living Rose!   O dowered with subtle dew
Of love, the tiny eternities of time,
Caught between flying seconds, are well filled
With these futilities of fragrant rhyme;
In Love's retort distilled,
In sunrays of fierce loathing purified,
In moonrays of pure longing tried,
And gathered after many moons of labour
Into the compass of a single day,
And wrought into continuous tune,[1]
One laughter with one langour for its neightbour.
One thought of winter with one word of June,
Muddled and mixed in mere dismay,
Chiselled with the cunning chisel of despair,
Found wanting, well aware
Of its own fault, even insistent
Thereon; some fragrance rare
Stolen from my lady's hair
Perchance redeeming now and then the distant
Fugitive tunes.

18.   Ah! Love! the hour is over!
The moon is up, the vigil overpast.
Call me to thee at last,
O Rose, O perfect miracle lover,
Call me!   I hear thee though it be across
The abyss of the whole universe,
Though not a sign escape, delicious loss!
Though hardly a wish rehearse
The imperfection underlying ever
The perfect happiness.
Thou knowest that not in flesh

---

[1] It will be noticed in fact that this poem is in the original metre, no stanza being complete in itself, but one running on into the next.

Lies the fair fresh
Delight of Love; not in mere lips and eyes
The secret of these bridal ecstasies,
Since thou art everywhere,
Rose of the World, Rose of the Uttermost
Abode of Glory, Rose of the High Host
Of heaven, mystic, rapturous Rose!
The extreme passion glows
Deep in this breast; thou knowest (and love knows)
How every word awakes its own reward
In a thought akin to thee, a shadow of thee;
And every tune evokes its musical Lord;
And every rhyme tingles and shakes in me
The filaments of the great web of Love.

19. O Rose all roses far above
In the garden of God's roses,
Sorrowless, thornless, passionate Rose, that lies
Full in the flood of its own sympathies
And makes my life one tune that curls and closes
On its own self delight;
A circle, never a line!   Safe from all wind,
Secure in its own pleasure-house confined,
Mistress of all its moods,
Matchless, serene, in sacred amplitudes
Of its own royal rapture, deaf and blind
To aught but its own mastery of song
And light, shown ever as silence and deep night
Secret as death and final.   Let me long
Never again for aught!   This great delight
Involves me, weaves me in its pattern of bliss,
Seals me with its own kiss,
Draws me to thee with every dream that glows,
Poet, each word! Maiden, each burden of snows
Extending beyond sunset, beyond dawn!
O Rose, inviolate, utterly withdrawn
In the truth:—for this is truth: Love knows!
Ah! Rose of the World!   Rose!   Rose!

II.
THE NIGHTMARE.

Up, up, my bride!   Away to ride
   Upon the nightmare's wings!
The livid lightning's wine we'll drink,
And laugh for joy of life, and think
   Unutterable things!

The gallant caught the lady fair
   Below the arms that lay
Curling in coils of yellow hair,
   And kissed her lips.   "Away!"

The lover caught his mistress up
   And lifted her to heaven,
Drank from her lips as from the cup
   Of poppies drowsed at even.

"Away, away, my lady may!
   The wind is fair and free;
Away, away, the glint of day
Is faded from the ghostly grey
   That shines beyond the sea."

The lordly bridegroom took the bride
   As giants grasp a flower.
"A night of nights, my queen, to ride
   Beyond the midnight hour."
The bride still slept; the lonely tide
   Of sleep was on the tower.

"Awake, awake! for true love's sake!
   The blood is pulsing faster.
My swift veins burn with keen desire
Toward those ebony wings of fire,
   The monarchs of disaster!"
The golden bride awoke and sighed
   And looked upon her master.

The bride was clad in spider-silk;
   The lord was spurred and shod.
Her breasts gleamed bright and white as milk.
   Most like the mother of God;
His heart was shrouded, his face was clouded,
   Earth trembled where he trod.

"By thy raven tresses; by those caresses
   We changed these five hours past;
By the full red lips and the broad white brow
I charge thee stay; I am weary now;
   I would sleep again—at last."

"By thy golden hair; by the laugher rare
   Of love's kiss conquering,
By the lips full red and the ivory bed
I charge thee come, I am fain instead
   Of the nightmare's lordly wing!"

The bride was sad and spoke no more.
   The tower erect and blind
Rocked with the storm that smote it sore,
   The thunder of the wind.

Swift to their feet the nightmare[1] drew
   And shook its gorgeous mane.
"Who rideth me shall never see
   His other life again.

"Who rideth me shall laugh and love
   In other ways than these."
"Mount, mount!" the gallant cried, "enough
   Of earthly ecstasies!"

The pale bride caught his colour then:
   The pale bride laughed aloud,
Fronting red madness in her den:
   "The bride-robe be my shroud!

"The bride-robe gave me light and clean
   To kisses' nuptial gold.
Now for a draught of madness keen!
   The other lips are cold."

They mount the tameless thundering side;
   They sweep toward the lea;
The mare is wild; they spur, they ride,
Mad master and hysteric bride,
   Along the lone grey sea.

---

[1] Night-mare has of course nothing to do with the horse, etymologically. Mare is from A.S. *mara*, an incubus.—A. C.

The pebbles flash, the waters shrink!
  (So fearful are those wings!)
The lightning stoops to let them drink.
They see each other's eyes, and think
  Unutterable things.

And now the sea is loose and loud;
  Tremendous the typhoon
Sweeps from the westward as a shroud,
Wrapping some great god in a cloud,
  Abolishing the moon.

And faster flying and faster still
  They gallop fast and faster.
"Turn, turn thy rein!" she shrieked again,
  "'Tis edged with sore disaster."
He looked her through with sight and will:—
  The pale bride knew her master.

And now the skies are black as ink,
  The nightmare shoreward springs;
The lightning stoops to let them drink.
They hold each other close, and think
  Unutterable things.

The roar of earthquake stuns the ear;
  The powers volcanic rise,
Casting the lava red and sheer
A million miles in ether clear
  Beyond the labouring skies.

Ghastlier faces bend around
  And gristlier fears above.
They see no sight: they hear no sound;
But look toward the hill profound
  End and abyss of love.

The water and the skies are fallen
  Far beyond sight of them.
All earth and fire grasp and expire:
The night hath lost her starry host,
  Shattered her diadem.

Eternity uplifts its brink
  To bar the wizard wings.
The lightning stoops to let them drink.

They silently espouse, and think
   Unutterable things.

The nightmare neighs!   The untravelled ways
   Are past on fervid feet.
The limits of the limitless
Flash by like jewels on a dress,
   Or dewdrops fallen in wheat.

"O love!   O husband!   Did you guess
   I did not wish to go?
And now—what rapture can express
   This?—do you feel and know?"
The girl's arms close in a caress;
   Her lips are warm aglow;
She looks upon his loveliness:—
The night has frozen the old stress;
   His mouth is cold as snow!

But closer to the corpse she links,
   And closer, closer clings.
Her kiss like lightning drops and drinks.
She burns upon his breast, and thinks
   Unutterable things.

Now half a moment stayed the steed;
   And then she thought he sighed;—
And then flashed forward thrice the old speed:—
   And then she knew he had died.

But close to him clings she yet,
   And feeds his corpse with fire,
As if death were not to forget
   And to annul desire.

And therefore as the utter space
   Sped past by hour and hour,
She feeds her face upon his face
   Like a bird upon a flower.

"Awake, awake! for love's own sake!
   I grow so faint and cold;
I charge thee by the bridal bed,
The violet veins, and the lips full red,
   And the hours of woven gold!"

And colder now the bride's lips grow
   And colder yet colder,
Until she lies as cold as snow,
   Her head against his shoulder.

The nightmare never checked its pace.
   The lovely pair are gone
Together through the walls of space
   Into oblivion.

III.
THE KISS

I BEHOLD in a mist of hair involving
Subtle shadows and shapes of ivory beauty.
Gray blue eyes from the sphered opal eyelids
Look me through and make me a deep contentment
Slow dissolving desire.   We sit so silent
Death might sweep over sleep with flowers of cypress
(Gathered myriad blossoms, Proserpina's),
Stir us not, nor a whisper steal through love trance.
Still we sit; and your head lies calm and splendid
Shadowed, curve of an arm about it whispering.
Still your bosom respires its sighs of silver;
Still one hand o' me quivers close, caresses.
Touches not.   O a breath of sudden sadness
Hides your face as a mist grows up a mountain!
Mist is over my eyes, and darkness gathers
Deep on violet inset deep of eyepits.
Neither holds in the sight the lovely vision.
Slow the mist is dissolved in the wintry sunlight
On the fells, and the heather wakes to laughter:—
So sight glimmers across the gulf of sorrow.
You the lily and I the rose redouble,
Bend, soft swayed by a slow spontaneous music,
Bend to kiss, are alight, one lamp of moon-rays
Caught, held hard in a crystal second.   Swiftly
Touch, just touch, the appealing floral sisters,
Brush no bloom off the blossom, lift no lip-gleam
Off the purple and rose, caressing cressets,
Flames of flickering love.   They draw asunder.
Thus, and motionless thus, for ages.   Hither!

IV.
ANNIE

ANEMONES grow in the wood by the stream;
   And the song of the spring in our garden
Wakes life to the shape of an exquisite dream;
   And reason of passion asks pardon.

I made up a posy by moonlight, a rose,
   And a violet white from its cranny,
And a bluebell, and stole, on the tips of my toes,
   At the dark of the night to my Annie.

Her window was open; she slept like a child;
   So I laid the three flowers on her breast,
And stole back alone through the forest deep aisled,
   To dream of the lass I loved best.

And the next night I lay half awake on my bed,
   When—a foot-fall as soft as the breeze!
Oh! never a word nor a whisper she said
   To distrub the low song of the trees.

But she crept to my side. Awhile we lay close:
   Then: "Have pardon and pity for me!"
She whispered—"your bluebell and violet and rose
   I can give but one flower for three."

V.
BRÜNNHILDE.[1]

THE sword that was broken is perfect: the hero is here
Be done with the dwarfs and be done with the spirit of fear!

Hark! the white note of a bird; and the path is declared;
The sword is girt on, and the dragon is summoned and dared.

Be down with the dragons! Awaits for the lord of the sword
On the crest of a mountain the maid, the availing award.

The spear of the Wanderer shivers, the God is exhaust.
Be done with the Gods! the key of Valhalla is lost.

The fires that Loki the liar built up of deceit
Are the roses that cushion the moss for the warrior's feet.

Be done with the paltry defences!   She sleeps.   O be done
With he mists of the mountain! Awake to the light of the sun!

Awake! Let the wave of emotions conflicting retire,
Let fear and despair be engulfed in delight and desire.

There is one thing of all that remains: that the sword may not bite:
It is love that is true as itself; and their scion, delight.

True flower of the flame of love: true bloom of the ray of the sword!
The lady is lost if she wit not the name of her lord.

Awaken and hither, O warrior maiden!   Above.
The Man is awaiting.   Be done with the lies!   It is love.

---

[1] See Wagner, from whose "Ring of the Nibelungs" the symbolism of this poem is taken.

VI.
DORA.

DORA steals across the floor
    Tiptoe;

Opens then her rosy door,
    Peeps out.

"Nobody!   And where shall I
    Skip to?"

Dora, diving daintily,
    Creeps out.

"To the woodland!   Shall I find
    Crowtoe,

Violet, jessamine!   I'll bind
    Garlands

Fancy I'm a princess.   Where
    Go to?

Persia, China, Finisterre?
    Far lands!"

Pity Dora!   Only one
    Daisy

Did she find.   The sulking sun
    Slept still.

Dora stamped her foot.   Aurora
    Lazy

Stirred not.   Hush!   A footstep.   Dora
    Kept still.

What a dreadful monster!   Shoot!
    Mercy!

('Twas a man.)   Suppose the brute
    Are her?

By-and-by the ruffian grows
    "Percy."

And she loves him now she knows
    Better.

VII.[1]
FATIMA.

FRAUGHT with the glory of a dead despair,
My purple eidola, my purple eidola
March, dance—through hyacinthine spheres
Moaning: they sweep along, attain, aware
How frail is Fatima.
They bathe the Gods with stinging tears.
They weave another thread within the mystic veil.
They are drawn up anon in some great hand.
They shudder and murmur in the web of Kama.
They hear no music in the white word Rama.
They rush, colossi, liquid swords of life
Strident with spurious desire and strife.
Mocked!   I am dumb: I await the gray command:
I wait for Her:
Inscrutable darkness through the storm
Loomed out, with broidered features of gold: its form
Wing-like lay on the firmaments,
River-like curves in all its movements
Swift from inertia of vast voids rolled, stirred
Gigantic for roar of strepitation: whirred The essential All
That was Her veil: her voice I had heard
Had not large sobbing fears surged; will and word Fall
Down from the black pearls of the night, down, back
      To night's impearlèd black;
Down, from chryselephantine wall
And rose-revolving ball.
Doomed, fierce through Saturn's aeons to tear,
Fraught with the glory of a dead despair.

---

[1] Written in collaboration with S. M.

VIII.
FLAVIA.

I KISSED the face of Flavia fair,
   In the deep wet dews of dawn,
And the ruddy weight of my lover's hair
Fell over me and held me there
   On the broad Italian lawn.

And the bright Italian moon arose
   And cleft the cypress grove;
For sadness in all beauty grows,
And sorrow from its master knows
   How to appear like love.

Alas! that Falvia's gentle kiss,
   And Flavia's cool caress,
And Flavia's flower of utter bliss
Must fade, must cease, must fall and miss
   The height of happiness.

The moon must set, the sun must rise,
   The wind of dawn is chill.
Oh, in this world of miseries
Is one hour's pleasure ill to prize?
   Is love the means of ill?

Oh, if there were a God to hear!
   Or Christ had really given
His life!   Or did a Dove appear
Bearing a rosebud, we might fear
   Or hope for hell or heaven.

Alas! no sign is given.   But short
   Bliss of the earth is ours;
The kiss that stops the avenging thought;
The furtive passion shrewdly caught
   Between the summer flowers.

So, Flavia, till the dawn awake
   Cling close, cling close, as this is!
While moonlight lingers on the lake,
Our present happiness we'll take
   And fill the night with kisses!

IX.
KATIE CARR.

'TWAS dark when church was out! the moon
  Was low on Rossett Ghyll;[1]
The organ's melancholy tune
  Grew subtle, far, and still.

All drest in black, her white, white throat
  Like moonlight gleamed; she moved
Along the road, towards the farm,
  Too happy to be loved.

"O Katie Carr! how sweet you are!"
  She only hurried faster:
She found an arm about her waist:
  A maiden knows her master.

Through grass and heather we walked together;
  So hard her heart still beat
She thought she saw a ghost, and fast
  Flickered the tiny feet.

"O Katie Carr, there's one stile more!
  For your sweet love I'm dying.
There's no one near; there's nought to fear."
  The lassie burst out crying.

"From Wastdale Head to Kirkstone Pass
  There's ne'er a lass like Kate:"—
The gentle child looked up and smiled
  And kissed me frank and straight.

The night was dark, the stars were few:—
  Should love need moon or star?
Let him decide who wins a bride
  The peer of Katie Carr.

---

[1] A pass in Cumberland.

X.
NORAH.

NORAH, my wee shy child of wonderment,
   You are sweeter than a swallow-song at dusk!
You are braver than a lark that soars and trills
   His lofty laughter of love to a hundred hills!
You lie like a sweet nut within the husk
   Of my big arms; and uttermost content
I have of you, my tiny fairy, eh?
   Do you live in a flower, I wonder, and sleep and pray
To the good God to send you dew at dawn
   And rain in rain's soft season, and sun betimes,
And all the gladness of the afterglow
   When you come shyly out of the folded bud,
Unsheath your dainty soul, bathe it in blood
   Of my heart?   Do you love me?   Do you know
How I love you?   Do you love these twittering rhymes
   I string you?   Is your tiny life withdrawn
Into its cup for modesty when I sing
   So softly to you and hold you in my hands,
You wild, wee wonder of wisdom?   Now I bring
   My lips to your body an touch you reverently,
Knowing as I know what Gabriel understands
   When he spreads his wings above for canopy
When you would sleep, you frail angelic thing
   Like a tiny snowdrop in its own life curled—
But oh! the biggest heart in all the world!

XI.
MARY.

MARY, Mary, subtle and softly breathing,
Look once eager out of the eyes upon me,
Draw one sigh, resign and abide in maiden
    Beauty for ever!

Love me, love me, love me as I desire it,
Strong sweet draughts not drawn of a well of passion,
Truth's bright crystal, shimmering out of sunlight
    Into the moon-dawn.

Closer cling, thou heart of amazed rapture,
Cords of starlight fashioned about thee net-wise,
Tendrils woven of gossamer twist about us!
    These be the binders!

Night winds whirl about the avenger city;
Darkness rides on desolate miles of moor-land;
Thou and I, desparted a little, part not
    Spirit from spirit.

Strange and sister songs in the middle ether
Grow, divide; they hover about, above us.
We, the song consummate of love, give music
    Back to the mortal.

Here, my love, a garden of spice and myrtle;
Sunlight shakes the rivers of love with laughter;
Here, my love, abide, in the amber ages,
    Lapped in the levin.

Linger, linger, light of the blessed moonrise!
Full-orbed sweep immaculate through the midnight!
Bend above, O sorrowful sister, kiss me
    Once and for ever!

Let the lake of thought be as still as darkmans[1]
Brooding over magian pools of madness!
Love, the sun, arise and abide above us,
    Mary Mavourneen.

---

[1] Night—an old English canting word.

XII.
XANTIPPE.

SWEET, do you scold?   I had rather have you scold
   Than from another earn a million kisses.
The tiger rapture on your skin's Greek gold
Is worth a million smiles of sunken cold
And Arctic archangelic passion rolled
   From any other woman.   Heaven misses
The half of God's delight who doth not see
   Some lightning anger dart like love and strike
Into the sacred heart its iterant glee
Of scathing tortures worth Hell's agony
To melt—ah, sweet, I know! in foam and free
Lustre of love redoubled.   Come to me!
   I will avenge the anger, like to like
With gentle fires of smitten love, will burn
   Into your beauty with the athletic rush
Of conquering godhead; and you cheek shall burn
   From red of wrath to shame's adorable blush,
And so in tears and raptures mix the cup
   Of dreadful wine we are wont to drain and—well!—
Needs but one glance to lift the liquor up,
   One angry grip to wake me, and to swell
The anguish into rapture—come, to sup
   The liquid lava of the lake of Hell!

XIII.
EILEEN.

THE frosty fingers of the wind; the eyes
Of the melancholy wind: the voice serene
Of the love-moved wind: the exulting secrecies
Of the subtle wind: lament, O harmonies
Of the most musical wind!   Eileen!

The peace of the nameless loch: the waiting heart
Of the amorous loch: the lights unguessed, unseen,
Of the midnight loch; the winter's sorrow apart
Of the ice-bound loch: O majesty of art
Of the most motionless loch!   Eileen!

The gleam of the hills: the stature of the hills
Facing the wind and the loch: the cold and clean
Sculpture of the stalwart hills; the iron wills
Of the inscrutable hills!   O strength that stills
The cry of the angonised hills!   Eileen!

Come back, O thought, alike from burn and ben
And sacred loch and rapture strong and keen
Of the wind of the moor.   A race of little men
Lives with the little.   The exalted ken
Knows the synthetic soul.   Eileen!

Close in the silence cling the patient eyes
Of love: the soul accepts her time of teen,
Awaits the answer.   Midnight droops and dies,
A floral hour; what dawn of love shall rise
On a world of sorrow?   Peace!   Eileen!

Mazed in a Titan world of rock and snow?
Horsed among the bearded Bedwain?
Drowsed on a tropic river in the glow
Of sunset?   Whither?   Who shall care or know,
When one and all are this?   Eileen!

XIV.

THE night is void of stars: the moon is full,
Veiling their radiance with her beautiful
Mist of still light.   O slumbrous air!
Wings of the winter, droop to-night!   Behold
The mirror of shuddering silver in the gold
Setting of loose involving hair!

Closer and closer through the dusk of sense
Avails the monotone omnipotence.
Steady, in one crescent tune,
Rises the virgin moon;
And from the depth of eyes flooded with love
Shines ecstasy thereof.

Words pass and are not heard.   The ear, awake
Only for its master's individual sake,
Strains only for three whispered songs,
Hears naught beside, interprets silence so,
Till liquid melodies of music flow
"I love you."   We afford to wait; who longs
That knows?   And we know; for the moon is full.

Steals in the ambient aura of delight
That quivering ray intense and cool
Self centred.   Woven of a million lines
There is a curve of light,
A pure, ideal curve, single, that shines
Amid the manifold night
Of all the flowery dreams that build it up.
So from the azure cup
Of heaven inverted is the white wine poured.
Stay, O thou vivid sword
Of soul, and cease, and be not!   Unto me
Through all eternity
Let me be not, and this thing be!

XV.

O THE deep wells and springs of tears!
O the intenser rays of blue,
Fleeting through gray unaltering spheres,
Like skies beholden through the dew!
O pearls of light!   O sombre meres
Wherein a waterwitch is hid,
And chants of sunset rise unbid,
Your eyes, your eyes!   They read me through,
Sphinx; and your soul, the Pyramid,
Burns upward, and I worship you.

2.

But had I moulded beauty's eyes
I had not touched the carving tool
Thus tenderly: my spirit dies
Before you, but my life still lies
Salient, unwounded, and to dule
Wakes: I had rather you were now
Medusa, of the awful brow,
The snaky hair, the face of fear.
So could I shout my eyes; feel how
Your hair fell back on me and bit,
Your lips descended on my face
In one exenterate kiss: and wit
I should abide a little space—
So little a space!—and solemn rise,
Face the black vaults of the alone,
And, knowing, lift to you mine eyes,
Look on your face, and turn to stone.

XVI.

THE schoolboy drudges through his Greek;
Plods to the integral calculus;
Makes sulphuretted hydrogen;

And, if the poor dumb thing could speak,
He'd say: Hic labor omnibus
Prodest: vitae verae limen.

Deinde missa juventute
Ave! cum otio dignitas![1]
So I: and stove and did not shirk.

But now? Confront me life and duty:
Toil is my daily hap, alas!
And work is still the sire of work.

Shall I repine? What joys are hid
In weariness of idleness?
Rich, young, beloved, shall I recede?

Enjoy? Not I! I work unbid;
Book follows book: ideas press
Hurrying over the green mead

Of mind: they roll, a rippling stream
Hurrying, hurrying: hour by hour
The brain throbs: shall I never rest?

Ay! for a little: peace supreme
Receives my head that lies a flower
Borne on the mountain of thy breast.

---

[1] This work is good for all men, the threshold of real life. Then, once youth is past, Hail! Ease and dignity.

XVII.

SPEAK, O my sister, O my spouse, speak, speak!
   Sigh not, but utter the intense award
Of infinite love; arise, burn cheek by cheek!
   Dart, eyes of glory; live, O lambent sword
O' the heart's gold rushing over mount and moor
   Of sunlit rapture! rise all runes above,
Dissolve thyself into one molten lure,
   Invisible core of the visible flame of love;
Heart of the sun of rapture, whirling ever;
   Strength of the sight of eagles, pierce the foam
Of ecstasy's irremeable river,
   And race the rhythm of laughter to its home
In the heart of the woman, and evoke the light
Of love out of the fiery womb of night!

XVIII.
FRIENDSHIP.

BETTER than bliss of floral kiss,
Eternal rapture caught and held;
Better than rapture's self is this
To which we find ourselves compelled,
The trick of self-analysis.

Thoughts fetter not true love: we weld
No bands by logic: on our lips
The idle metaphysic quibble
Laughs: what portends the late eclipse?
What oracle of the solar sybil?

Orion's signal banner dips:
"This is the folly of your youth,
Achieving the exalted aim;
Because you have gained a higher truth
To call it by a lower name."

XIX.

Rose on the breast of the world of spring, I press my breast against thy bloom,
My subtle life drawn out to thee: to thee its moods and meanings cling.
I pass from change and thought to peace, woven on love's incredible loom,
Rose on the breast of the world of spring!

How shall the heart dissolved in joy take form and harmony and sing?
How shall the ecstasy of light fall back to music's magic gloom?
O China rose without a thorn, O honey-bee without a sting!

The scent of all thy beauty burns upon the wind.   The deep perfume
Of our own love is hidden in our hearts, the invulnerable ring.
No man shall know.   I bear thee down unto the tomb, beyond the tomb,
Rose on the breast of the world of spring!

XX.

LIE still, O love, and let there be delight!
Lie on the soft banks of ambrosial air,
The roseate marble of invisible space.
Secure and silent, O caressing night,
We are in thee; and thou art everywhere.
Lie still, and read thy soul upon my face.

Swayed slowly by the wind, made craftsmen of
The mystery of happiness, we lie
And rock us to and fro, and to and fro.
Shrined in the temple of the world, O love,
We wait self-worshipped through eternity,
Until "to ignore" is equal to "to know."

Lie still, O love, and let me hide my brows
In the deep bosom and the scented vales.
Thy deep drawn breath embrace my hair, resume
My life in thine!   Here is an amber house
With gateways of old gold.   Far nightingales
Sing like smooth silence through the extreme perfume.

Moving, flying, exulting, on we go,
Borne on blue clouds of glory.   On the river,
Over the mountains of the night, above
The stars of the night, above the floral glow
Of the sun dawning now for us for ever
Who rest content in the abode of love!

Lie still, O love, and let the fragrant sleep
Perfume our eyelids with dew-dropping death,
And silence be the witness of the will.
Fall, fall, fall back in the uprolling deep
Wrapt in rose mist of unsuccessive breath
Of love, of love.   Lie still, O love, lie still.

XXI.

UNDER the stars the die was cast to win.
The moonrays stained with pale embroidered bars
The iridescent shimmer of your skin,
          Under the stars.

Great angels drove their pearl-inwoven cars
Through the night's racecourse: silence stood within
The folded cups of passion's nenuphars.

You were my own; sorrowless, without sin,
That night—this night.　　Sinks the red eye[1] of Mars;
The hand of Hermes guides us as we spin
          Under the stars.

---

[1] Tibetan astrologers give these symbols to the planets Mars and Mercury.

XXII.

DROOP the great eyelids purple-veined!
Stand, pure and pale and tremulous!
Dare to believe, O soul unstained,
The truth unguessed and unexplained!

The unquiet air monotonous
Wreathes the sad head in whirring mist.
Hath the delicate will disdained
The delicate lips that would be kissed?

Like far blue snows by sunrise caught
Love lights the enlightened eyes of blue.
Dare to believe the child-heart's thought,
And wake in wonder!   For I knew
From the first hour that this was true.

XXIII.
PROTOPLASM.

ALTHOUGH I cannot leave these bitter leas,
And whisper wiser than the southern breeze,
And mix my master music with the sea's;

Although I shiver and you smile; heap coal
And you stand laughing where the long waves roll;
There is a sympathy of soul to soul.

Not Scylla, not the iron Symplegades
Shall bar that vessel, in delighted ease
Winning her way by stainless sorceries.

Though I be melancholy and thou fair,
And I be dark and thou too high for care;
Both yet may strive in serener air,

Clasping the vast, the immeasurable knees;
Searching the secrets of the calm decrees
Of Hermes gray or gold Musagetes!

Is there another?   Unprofane, aware,
See me secreted, silent, everywhere.
And then consider!   Dos thou dare to dare?

The live sun leaps by invisible degrees;
The blessèd moon grows slowly through the trees;
And fire has fire's ingressive agonies.

I everywhere abide, and I control
Olympian glories and the Pythian goal.
What isle unfurls yonder life's glimmering scroll?

This be thy shrine, and all its splendours these!
Awake to dream!   Two desolate nudities
Woven through sculpture into ecstasies.

XXIV.

AUM!   I unfold the tinted robe,
My love's embroideries one by one,
Unveil her glories, globe on globe,
And find beneath the quivering probe
    A shaking skeleton.

The smile of vermeil lips is past;
The skull's black grin awhile remains;
The fallen flesh desplays aghast
Ribbed bars of bone: was Venus cast
    For this?   What Mars attains?

Where is the poesy that shed
Its dewfall downward through her eys?
Gaunt sockets stare from bony head.
Moves she?   Ah me! the living dead!
    The poet loves?   He lies.

Others perceive thee, peerless maid
Broidered with beauty, starred and gemmed
With purity and light, arrayed
In wit—like moonlight down a glade
    With flowers diademed.

But I remember; see the form
Serene sink slowly to the dust.
'Tis but a date: the eventful storm
Comes: then or now?   What odds?   They swarm,
    The winds: this breath, one gust.

Ah! in the spiritual soul
Is there no essence to abide
When flesh and bone alike shall roll
From shape to shape, from goal to goal,
    On time, the envious tide?

All tire, all break, all pass.   Beware
False thirst, false trust, false doubts of truth
Whilst thou art young, whilst thou art fair,
Awake and see the sepulchre
    For beauty yawn and youth.

Strive to cessation.   Only this
I the true refuge: this alone
Be implicit in our subtle kiss,

Be master of the imperfect bliss
   We call perfection's throne.

Then, if we strive, not all in vain
This vision of the barrèd bones;
This knowledge in a poet's brain,
Daring to sing its own deep pain
   In shapeless semitones.

Ah! if we strive, we attain.   In sooth,
The effort is of old begun,
Or I had hardly seen the truth
Beneath thy beauty and thy youth:—
   A mouldering skeleton!

XXV.

I AM so sad and, being alone to-night,
I will not see you.   Self-disdain forbids.
I wander through the icy hermitage
Of the populous streets, hoping.   O might
Some idle God look through his drowsy lids
And will us happiness!   Serene and sage
Therefore I sit, as if I loved you not,
And train a practised pen, and strive to art;
Accomplish art, and lose the art therein.
I sit, a bitter Witenagemot,[1]
The saint, the poet, the man: the lover's heart
Pleads at the bar.   How should he hope to win?
The saint is silent while the poet strings
These futile follies, gives for bread a stone,
and the man endures.   The lover breaks the lyre.
Its death-cry, agony, O agony! rings
One name. The love sits in hell alone
Fondling the devil that men call desire.

---

[1] The ancient parliament of Britain.

XXVI.

WHEN the wearily falling blossom of midnight
Stirs the face of a sleeper, Mother of Sorrow!
Look thou down in the dawn of heavier dewfall.
Tears of widow despair, O mutely lamenting
Crouched in heavenly bowers over the carven
Gateway's ivory flower, tears of revival
Fall, oh fall, to the black abodes of the lonely.
I await, I await, I sing not for sorrow,
Train the fugitive lights of music across me,
Seek by force to avail me, vainly attempting
Song with feather detested, agony futile:
Ply these piteous exercises of cunning,
Hateful—ay! to myself!   To me it were better
Only to woo in the silence, magical silence,
Silence eloquent, wert thou here or afar, love.
Woo thee, nay! but abide in certain recession;
Stilled to the splendid currents fervid of passion;
Float to seas of an unassailable silence
Down the river of love.   The words are awakened:
Let the soul be asleep.   The dawn is upon us.

XXVII.[1]

Ecstasy, break through poetry's beautiful barriers,
Intricate webs, labyrinthine mazes of music!
Leap, love, lightning's self, and, athwart the appalling
Evil clouds of an agony bound by existence,
Enter, avail me, exult!   In the masses of matter
Nothing avails; in the splendour spirit is, nothing.
Give me love; I am weary of giants colossal,
Royal, impossible things; I am fain of a bosom
Always breathing sleep, and the symphony, silence.
Years are forgotten; abide, deep love, I am happy.

[1] An acrostic.

XXVIII.

COULD ivory blush with a stain of the sunset on highlands
    Of snow: could the mind of me span
The tenderness born of the dew in immaculate islands
    Virgin of maculate man:
Could I mingle the Alps and Hawaii; Strath Ness and A'pura[1] and Baiae;
    Kashmir and Japan:

Could lilies attain to the life of the Gods; could a comet
    Attain to the calm of the moon:
I would mingle them all in a kiss, and draw from it
    The soul of a sensitive tune.
All lovers should hear it and know it: not needing the words of a poet
    In ebony hewn.

O beam of discovery under the eyelids awaking
    The sense of delight!   O assent
Slow dawning through cream into roses!   O white bosom shaking
    The myrtles of magical scent
In the groves of the heart!   O the pleasure that runs over all overmeasure,
    The wine of Event!

Overmastered the hurl of the world in the hush of our rapture;
    Entangled the bird of success
In the snare of bewildering fancies.   We capture
    Delight in the toils of a tress
Rough gilded of sunlight and umber with virginal shadows of slumber—
    Ah! sorrow, regress!

Till the idle abyss of eternity swoon to our pinions
    With music of wings as we fly
Through the azure of dreams, and the purple of mighty dominions
    Exalted, afoam in the sky;
And to us it were wiser and sweeter to ruin the race of the metre,
    And song were to die.

---

[1] Anuradapura, the ruined sacred city of Ceylon.

Printed in Great Britain
by Amazon